I0844973

Lion

Tiger

Leopard

Fox

Wolf

Husky

Elephant

Rhinoceros

Hippo

Bison

Zebra

Giraffe

Elk

Lama

Monkey

Gorilla

Kangaroo

Squirrel

Meerkat

Bear

Hedgehog

Panda

Owl

Bald Eagle

Falcon

Mallard

Bat

Seal

Sea Turtle

Tusk

Penguin

Polar Bear

Horse

Donkey

Bull

Cow

Goat

Sheep

Chicken

Turkey

Duck

Goose

Rabbit

Pig

Cat

Dog